Weird & Wacky
Creatures

K.B. Carr

The Weird & Wacky Planet Series

This edition published in 2016 by Weird & Wacky Planet and DSG Publishing, Greenville, MI 49546

Printed in USA

Book cover and interior designed by Kelsey Leigh (Yes, that Kelsey) www.IamKelseyLeigh.com

Publisher's Cataloging-in-Publication Data
provided by Five Rainbows Cataloging Services

Names: Carr, K. B. | Leigh, Kelsey, illustrator.
Title: Weird & wacky creatures : strange, weird animals that really exist! / K.B. Carr ; [illustrated by] Kelsey Leigh.
Description: Greenville, MI: DSG Publishing, 2017. | Series: Weird & wacky planet. | Previously published in 2015. | Includes bibliographical references and index. | Summary: Out there, somewhere in the world, are weird creatures who could very easily be aliens from other planets, but they share the same Earth we do. | 5th & 6th grades.
Identifiers: LCCN 2015953151 | ISBN 978-0-9968375-1-4 (pbk.) | ISBN 978-0-9968375-0-7 (ebook)
Subjects: LCSH: Animals--Miscellanea--Juvenile literature. | Curiosities and wonders--Juvenile literature. | Exotic animals--Juvenile literature. | Children's questions and answers. | BISAC: JUVENILE NONFICTION / Animals / General. | JUNENILE NONFICTION / Science & Nature / Zoology. | JUVNILE NONFICTION / Curiosities & Wonders. | JUVENILE NONFICTION / Science & Nature / Environmental Conservation & Protection.
Classification: LCC QL49 .C32 2017 (print) | LCC QL49 (ebook) | DDC590--dc23.

THIS BOOK IS DEDICATED TO:

The many rescue and conservation organizations who help creatures everywhere, and to whom part of the proceeds of this book are donated. To learn more about how you can help, please visit the resource page at www.KBCarr.com.

And, to Val,
who believed enough to put her money where her mouth is.
I will be eternally grateful!

And finally, to Ryan & Kelsey,
who are-and always will be-
my favorite Weird & Wacky Creatures.

Weird & Wacky Planet is da bomb diggity. Stick your neck out and read a few...

AT THE WEIRD & WACKY PLANET WEBSITE, YOU CAN :

Vote for other books you want to see-
Learn about how to get a FREE eBook-
Join the Weird & Wacky Planet Conservation Kids Club-
Purchase Conservation Club Adventurer's Kits & other fun merch-
See fun videos-
Read the Random Stuff blog-
See cute pictures of Captain Jack-
Find all the newest W&W books-
Learn more about K.B.-
& Contact K.B. and Captain Jack.

To access the FREE bonus downloads, go to the Thank You page in the back of this book!

OTHER BOOKS IN THIS SERIES

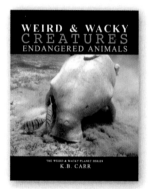
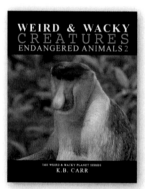
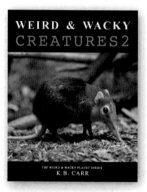

TABLE OF CONTENTS

FOR PARENTS AND TEACHERS

This book has been written with the reluctant reader in mind. It will hopefully spark a child's natural curiosity, improving reading comprehension, as well as spelling skills. Another worthy goal is to foster an interest in science, especially for girls.

Kids can also use it as an educational reference tool. They will have the ability to write a full page report on each animal with the information given. Each chapter includes the scientific name, other names the animal may have, species classification, IUCN status, biome, food source, physical facts, and of course, what makes the animal so fascinating-the weird and wacky part!

All the informational resources are listed in the Resource section so that facts can be verified and expanded. There is a Glossary in the back with the terms underlined throughout the book. This meets the Common Core Educational State Standard Initiative, teaching children to look up words they may not be familiar with. If any photographs are used from this book, the photographers ask that credit be given to them. The photo attributions are listed in the Resources and Photo Credit section.
Teaching Aids are available for each book at www.WeirdandWackyPlanet.com.

Part of the proceeds for this book go to support rescue and conservation organizations.
Kids can learn early on that they have a stake in how our planet operates, and wildlife conservation can be an excellent place to start. Our custodianship of Earth will eventually be turned over to them, and encouraging concern about the status of the creatures we share the world with is part of the education we can leave them. The next generation of custodians should be as prepared and as enthusiastic as possible, because, as we well know, it's a very big job. :)

-KBC

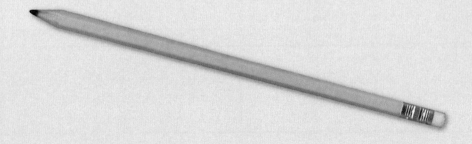

INTRODUCTION

Is truth stranger than fiction?

Out there, somewhere in the world, are weird creatures that could very easily be aliens from other planets, but they share the same Earth we do. These creatures are so weird and so wacky that I felt compelled to write about them, and what's more, there are so many of them, I couldn't fit them all in one book!

Some of them you've heard of, but you may not know everything that makes them weird and wacky. Others, you may never have heard of and you may have a hard time believing they really exist, but I assure you they do, and I have the pictures to prove it.

Because some of these animals are on the Endangered Species list according to the IUCN, which stands for the International Union for Conservation of Nature, I have included their status on that list.

The IUCN Status categories are as follows:
DD - Not Enough Information
EX - Extinct
EW - Extinct in the Wild
CR - Critically Endangered
EN - Endangered
VU - Vulnerable
NT - Near Threatened
LC - Least Concern

You can also use this book to write a report on any animal in here, because I have included the scientific name, along with any other names it might be called, as well as its classification. I've included the region of the world where it's located, biome, what it eats, and regular facts about it, such as size and physical description. And, of course, why it's Weird & Wacky!

The other thing I do is donate a portion of the sales from every book, T-shirt, Decal, and Adventure Kit to rescue and conservation organizations, because they fight every day against animal extinction. If you want more information about how you can help, check out the resouce page on the website. And, if you want to take a look at the Weird & Wacky Planet stuff, you can check it out at www.WeirdandWackyPlanet.com/Store.

You will find fun activities related to each animal in the Field Activity sections of the book. You can identify what different mole hills mean, tell the temperature by listening to a cricket's chirp, or make a piggy bank out of a soda bottle.

You may also notice there are dog prints here and there throughout the book. My daughter Kelsey, thought it would be fun to have my dog, Jack's paw prints in the book. We made a special page on the website where you can read the story of how my son, Ryan, rescued Jack off the streets and brought her home to me. She was the best Birthday present ever! You can find her story if you click on our picture on the home page. It's a hidden page only found if you know where to look. There are a few of those in here!

You will also find many underlined words in every chapter. At the back of the book, there are definitions for the underlined words, in case it's a new word for you, or you aren't quite sure what it means. Be sure to impress your family and friends with your new vocabulary. I love doing that!

But, I'm sure the part you'll be most interested in is the page about why these animals are in this book in the first place.

So, read on, because within these pages are some of the weirdest and wackiest creatures on the planet, proving once and for all, that truth really CAN be stranger than fiction!

Let the adventure begin...

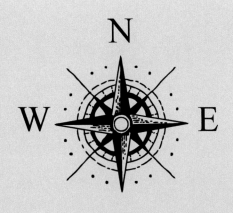

Put on your Adventurer's hat, get out your Field Journal, & get ready to dive into the world of

Weird & Wacky Creatures

Your adventure begins NOW!

Star Nosed Mole

[stahr-nohzd mohl]

FLOWER-FACED LAWN WRECKER

Mole prints

Yay! Mole Babies!

Close up of the Mole's flower-like nose. Pretty? Or pretty gross?

A Star Nosed Mole is emerging from its tunnel. And, if the nose wasn't drawing enough attention, SOMEONE also needs a manicure.

SCIENTIFIC NAME:
Condylura cristata

OTHER NAMES:
None

SPECIES CLASSIFICATION:
Mammal

IUCN STATUS:
LC - Least Concern

BIOME:
Region: North America
Habitat: Forests, lakes, ponds, rivers, marshes, and swamps
Range: Eastern Canada and Northeastern USA

DIET CLASSIFICATION:
Carnivore

FOOD SOURCE:
Small invertebrates, aquatic insects, worms, mollusks, small amphibians, and small fish

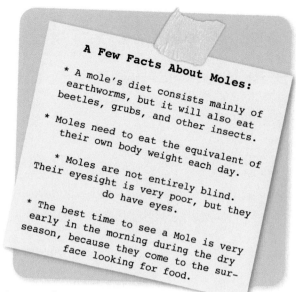

A Few Facts About Moles:

* A mole's diet consists mainly of earthworms, but it will also eat beetles, grubs, and other insects.
* Moles need to eat the equivalent of their own body weight each day.
* Moles are not entirely blind. Their eyesight is very poor, but they do have eyes.
* The best time to see a Mole is very early in the morning during the dry season, because they come to the surface looking for food.

ANIMAL FACTS:

* The Star Nosed Mole is about 6 to 8 inches long, which is about the size of a Hamster. Its blackish-brown fur is thick and water repellent. Its feet are big and scaled, and the front feet have large digging claws. The tail is long and thick. The Mole weights about 2 ounces, and has 44 teeth. I'm not sure why that's relevant, except that maybe people think it eats with its flower nose, but no...it has teeth.

* It gets around by tunneling, swimming and digging. Its natural enemies are Owls and Hawks from the air, Cats, Dogs, Skunks, Weasels, and Fox on the ground, and Bullfrogs and Large Mouth Bass in the water. Wow, it seems like no place is safe!

* They live about 3 or 4 years. That's assuming they escape all the animals trying to eat them.

* The female gives birth to a litter of 2 to 7 offspring per year, which is a good thing, considering ALL THE THINGS TRYING TO EAT THEM!

WHAT MAKES THEM WEIRD & WACKY?

The Star Nosed Mole's most distinctive feature is a large circle of twenty-two mobile, pink, fleshy <u>tentacles</u> called rays at the end of the snout, from which it derives its name.
Mobile means they move.

Think about that a minute. Yeah.

These <u>tentacles</u> are used to identify food by touch, such as worms, insects and <u>crustaceans</u>. The <u>tentacles</u> are extremely sensitive, and covered with tiny touch receptacles called Eimer's Organs. The nose is about one and a half inches in diameter, but has almost twenty-five thousand Eimer's Organs distributed over the twenty-two <u>tentacles</u>.

The Star Nosed Mole is functionally blind, and its nose is thought to be its prime finder of food. It also has been called the fastest eating <u>mammal</u> on the planet, taking as short a time as one hundred and twenty milliseconds to identify and consume its food.
Wow, talk about gulping down your dinner!

Moles are best known for tunneling underground and leaving long furrows in peoples' lawns, but these particular moles can also tunnel underwater. Star Nosed Moles are also able to SMELL underwater. They do this by exhaling air bubbles on to objects for scent trails and then inhaling the bubbles to carry scents back through the nose.
Super odd, but probably really handy for finding food underwater, right? It definitely gets my vote for the weirdest nose in the world.

Weirdest and kind of pretty...but, pretty in a weird kind of way...

THE GREAT MOLE RESCUE!

I once rescued a Star Nosed Mole out of my neighbor's dried up swimming pool! Well, it wasn't completely dried up, because there was some water in the deep end. In that water, several frogs and toads had come to live and raise their babies. The water was full of small frogs and tadpoles in various stages of development. I'm pretty sure that's what attracted the Mole in the first place. I put a rake down in the shallow end, hoping the Mole would use it to climb out, but he was still there the next day. Remember, Moles are functionally blind. I knew a Hawk or an Owl would get him if I didn't get him out of there, so I climbed down into the pool and picked him up with winter gloves on. Then I went back up to the house, grabbed my iPad and made a little video of him. It was the first video I ever made, so it wasn't very good, but you can see his star nose!

FIELD ACTIVITY
Related to a Starfish Nosed Rodent

Did you know that you can tell what Moles are doing by observing what kinds of Mole Hills they're making?

HERE'S HOW:

Large Mole Hills mark the position of a nest.

A line of small Mole Hills marks the direction of a deep tunnel.

A continuous line or row of dirt marks a very shallow tunnel.

What are the Moles in your yard up to?

Go have a
Mole Watching Adventure in YOUR neighborhood!

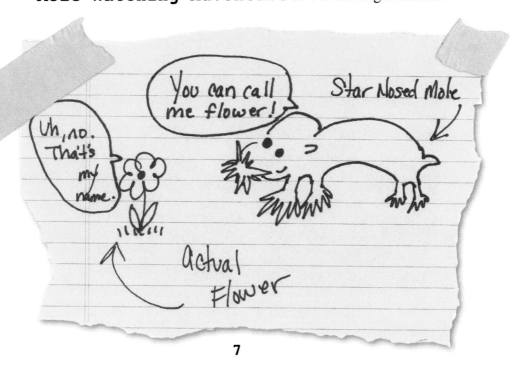

Babirusa

[bab-uh-roo-suh]

BECAUSE YOU CAN'T HAVE TOO MANY TUSKS

Don't hate me just because I'm beautiful...

Wild Boar Prints

This Babirusa is smelling around for food.

Because that's how Pigs roll.

SCIENTIFIC NAME:
Babyrousa celebensis

OTHER NAMES:
Deer Pig (Weird.)

SPECIES CLASSIFICATION:
Mammal

IUCN STATUS:
VU – Vulnerable

BIOME:
    Region: Indonesia
    Habitat: Tropical rain forests and riverbanks
    Range: Islands of Sulawesi, Togian, Sula, and Buru

DIET CLASSIFICATION:
Omnivore

FOOD SOURCE:
Leaves, roots, fruits, as well as fish and small mammals.

Mom is watching her babies play. Or fight. Awww...

ANIMAL FACTS:

* The Babirusa is a type of wild boar that is native to Indonesia. It appears to be bald, but actually has short hair. Its skin is a brownish-gray color.

* It is smaller than domestic pigs, but has longer deer-like legs. I suppose that's where the whole Deer Pig thing came from. I still think it's a weird name, though.

* The biggest ones are about 2 1/2 to 3 1/2 feet in length and weigh from 130 to 225 pounds. That is still a pretty substantial porker.

* Male Babirusas live in solitude, while females live in community groups. Unlike domesticated pigs, the female Babirusa only gives birth to one or two piglets at a time.

* Their lifespan is about ten years in the wild, but up to twenty years in captivity.

WHAT MAKES THEM WEIRD & WACKY?

The Babirusa has two sets of tusks-the upper <u>canines</u>, which grow up and curve over the face, and the lower <u>canines</u>, which also grow upwards.
The lower tusks are smaller, but the upper tusks can reach seventeen inches long.

But, here's the kicker-
No one knows what the tusks are for! They don't need them for food. And, they don't use them for defense. The male Babirusas fight by BOXING each other with their front hooves, like kangaroos.

I'd like to see a video of that, for sure. I guess those tusks are just there for good looks.

The Babirusa has a pig body, deer-like legs, has a two-chambered stomach like a sheep, and chews its cud like a cow. That's pretty weird, right?

But, here's something weirder...
If the Babirusa doesn't grind down its own tusks, they can keep growing, and eventually pierce the animal's own skull!

That's when getting lazy about grooming can kill you.

PERSONAL HYGIENE FAILS

These pictures show what happens when Babirusas don't take care of their teeth. Make sure you take care of yours!

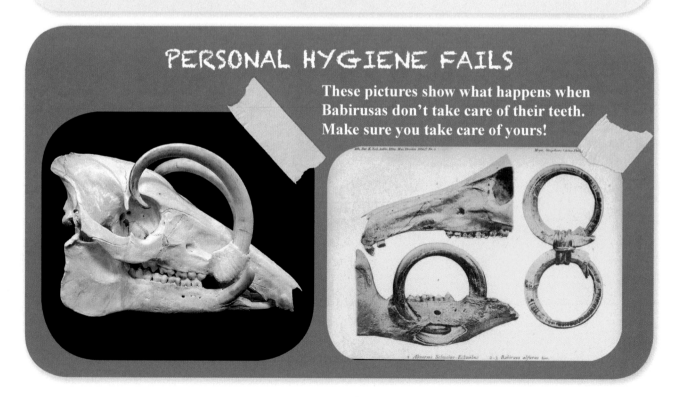

FIELD ACTIVITY

Related to the Curly Toothed Cow Pig
(a better nickname than Deer Pig, if I do say so myself)

Since Babirusas are mostly considered wild pigs, I thought I'd make this activity a Piggy-type project. What's a more useful thing to make than a Piggy Bank? Plus, I like the fact that it's made out of recycled materials. Instead of buying something new, we can make something out of things that we already have-things we might normally throw away. When we Recycle, Reduce, and Reuse, this means less garbage in our landfills and it's better for our Planet!

HERE'S WHAT YOU'LL NEED:

* 2 liter soda bottle
* Used wrapping paper or extra fabric
* Plastic eyes or draw your own!

* 5 bottle caps
* Glue & clear tape
* Black marker

Using an empty, clean 2 liter soda bottle, wrap your chosen paper/fabric around the middle part and secure it with a piece of tape. Cut out the ears and tail from the left over wrapping paper or fabric and glue on to bottle in the appropriate places. You can even use the white side of the paper for the front and a smaller piece of the colored side for the inside of the ears, if you want to get fancy. Glue four of the bottle caps to the bottom for feet. Screw on the remaining bottle cap and draw two nostrils on it for your pig's nose. Carefully cut, or have an adult cut, a slot to put your money in on top of the pig's back. You may also choose to make a trap door underneath the tail so you can get to your money if you need to. Or not, if you think you'll save more if you can't get to it so quickly. That's what I did!

Go have a **Swine Saving Adventure** in YOUR neighborhood!

Okapi
[oh-kah-pee]

DRESSED AS A ZEBRA FOR HALLOWEEN

Hoof prints

An Okapi wearing its awesome costume. Now, that's a horse of a different color!

SCIENTIFIC NAME:
Okapia johnstoni

OTHER NAMES:
Forest Zebra

SPECIES CLASSIFICATION:
Mammal

IUCN STATUS:
EN – Endangered

BIOME:
    Region: Central Africa
    Habitat: Dense Mountain Rainforest
    Range: Limited to the Ituri Rainforest because of natural barriers

DIET CLASSIFICATION:
Herbivore

FOOD SOURCE:
Leaves, shoots, and fruit

This Okapi is reaching for leaves with its tongue.

ANIMAL FACTS:

* The Okapi is a deer-like animal that weighs about five hundred pounds, and has a red, brown, black and white coat. It stands about five to six and a half feet tall. So...that's a pretty big, tall deer.

* But, it's also a very shy animal, and is rarely seen by humans. It is hunted by Leopards and Servals (another kind of big cat), and it runs about thirty-seven miles per hour, so I bet it's not that hard for a predator to run it down in open spaces.

* That's why it likes to stay in the thickest areas of the Rainforest and why humans don't see many of them.

* It has another defense as well, but you'll see that in the Weird and Wacky section.

* The Okapi lives for about twenty to thirty years and has one calf every one and a half to two years. It lives a <u>solitary</u> lifestyle, probably because there isn't a lot of room in a dense thicket. And maybe it's also shy of other Okapi, who knows?

WHAT MAKES THEM WEIRD & WACKY?

The biggest defense the Okapi has is its coloring. All those different colors and patterns help it blend in with the surrounding forest, so <u>predators</u> have a hard time seeing it.

The Okapi looks like it is part Zebra about halfway down. But, it isn't related to the Zebra at all.

It is, instead, one of the last remaining ancestors of the Giraffe!   WHAAAAT?!

Some of its Giraffe-like tendencies include its fighting habits. The males fight over territory, females, and who knows what else, by BASHING their necks together, just like Giraffes do. And where a Giraffe has a long, snaky, purplish-black tongue, the Okapi does, too.

It can actually wash its face and even clean out its own ears with its tongue.

That's just gross, right? Ewww...

Also, like their distant Giraffe relatives, Okapis can reach out and GRAB leaves with their tongues, just like a monkey's tail! The word for that is "<u>prehensile</u>". Now, that IS weird.

Or handy, depending on your perspective...

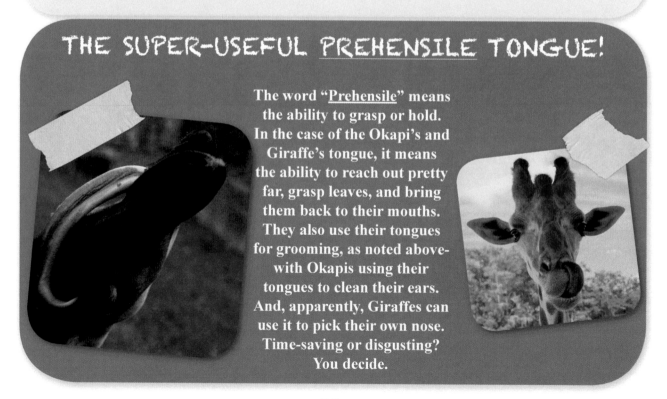

THE SUPER-USEFUL <u>PREHENSILE</u> TONGUE!

The word "<u>Prehensile</u>" means the ability to grasp or hold. In the case of the Okapi's and Giraffe's tongue, it means the ability to reach out pretty far, grasp leaves, and bring them back to their mouths. They also use their tongues for grooming, as noted above- with Okapis using their tongues to clean their ears. And, apparently, Giraffes can use it to pick their own nose. Time-saving or disgusting? You decide.

FIELD ACTIVITY

Related to an Animal with the Cleanest Ears in the Forest

I think an Okapi looks like several different animals all patched together, so I decided to take pictures of the other animals, cut them up, and paste them together to make my own Okapi. You can make one, too!

HERE'S WHAT YOU'LL NEED:

Pictures of a Horse, Giraffe, and a Zebra. You can either cut them out of magazines, draw them yourself, or download them from www.WeirdandWackyPlanet.com. Then, go nuts! You can make any combo of them you want to. You can stay traditional or make up an entirely different animal. I did both. Check out my results below:

Go have an
Creature Creating Adventure
in YOUR neighborhood!

My homemade "Okapi".

This one is weird.
But I like his hair :)

Liger

[lahy-ger]

A CAT'S CAT. LITERALLY.

Pretty Kitty!

A Liger husband is laughing at a joke his wife told him. I hope.

Lion print

Tiger print

SCIENTIFIC NAME:
Panthera leo, Panthera tigris

OTHER NAMES:
World's biggest cat

SPECIES CLASSIFICATION:
Mammal

IUCN STATUS:
None

BIOME:
Kept in captivity, either in Zoos, Shows, Exhibits, or Animal Sanctuaries.

DIET CLASSIFICATION:
Carnivore

FOOD SOURCE:
Raw meats given by Keepers.

Who's a beautiful boy?
This guy is!

ANIMAL FACTS:

* The Liger is the world's largest cat, weighing in at a whopping eight hundred to thirteen hundred pounds. Its fur is tan, black, brown, and orange. An average sized male can reach nine to twelve feet when standing on his hind legs.

* They are WAY taller than the tallest basketball player!

* Their lifespan is around twenty years, and the average litter size is two to four cubs. But, because of hybridization, the male Liger is unable to father cubs and offspring are rare and often unhealthy.

* What is hybridization? Read on...

WHAT MAKES THEM WEIRD & WACKY?

<u>Hybridization</u> is a mix of two species. The Liger is a <u>hybrid</u>, because it is a mix of a Lion and a Tiger!

It has the strength of a Lion and the speed of a Tiger.

The Liger mostly has the traits of a Lion, but one of the Tiger traits it has is a love of water. Lions don't like the water, but Ligers are excellent swimmers. They're also pretty good runners and can clock around fifty miles per hour.

There are no Ligers in the wild, because Lion and Tiger <u>habitats</u> don't overlap. The only way to get a Liger is by accident or deliberately breeding them in <u>captivity</u>. However, breeding them has been banned in most zoos and animal sanctuaries because of the health issues they face.

And get this: to be a Liger, the father has to be a Lion and the mother has to be a Tiger. If the father is a Tiger and the mother is a Lion, then the <u>offspring</u> is a Tigon, and is only half the size of the parents.
Weird, right?

Lions, and Tigers, and Ligers, Oh My.....

HERCULES, THE FAMOUS LIGER!

Jungle Island in Miami, is home to a Liger named Hercules [hur-kyuh-leez], the largest Liger in the world! He holds the Guinness Book of World Records as the largest living cat on Earth, weighing 922 pounds. Hercules has been featured on the Today Show, Good Morning America, Anderson Cooper 360, and Inside Edition. When he was only three years old, he already weighed 900 pounds! Hercules is about 10 years old, healthy, and is expected to live a long life. The longest living Liger on record lived to be 24.

FIELD ACTIVITY
Related to a Water-Loving Cool Cat

<u>Hybrid</u> animals are not a new concept. In fact, there are many of them! Maybe even enough to write a whole other book about them. Weird & Wacky <u>Hybrid</u> Creatures-Coming Soon! What do you think? I think yes! But, in the meantime, here are some other <u>Hybrids</u> that I made up. You can make your own <u>Hybrids,</u> too.

HERE'S WHAT YOU'LL NEED:

Pictures of animals, as many as you can find. Then, just start imagining what they would look like if you combined them! Just like in the Okapi chapter, what parts would go where? What would you call them? Here are a couple ones I made.

Go have a **Wild <u>Hybrid</u> Adventure**
in YOUR neighborhood!

It's a Tibear.

And, this is a Fruman.

Tarsier Monkey

[tahr-see-er muhng-kee]

MY, WHAT BIG EYES YOU HAVE!

Female
Orangutan print

Male
Orangutan print

A Tarsier Monkey sitting in a tree,
k-i-s-s-i-n-g bugs. And, then eating them.

SCIENTIFIC NAME:
Carlito syrichta, Tarsius

OTHER NAMES:
Eastern, Western, or Philippine Tarsier, Maomag

SPECIES CLASSIFICATION:
Mammal

IUCN STATUS:
CR – Critically Endangered

BIOME:
> Region: Islands of Southeast Asia
> Habitat: Forests, Mangroves, and Scrub
> Range: Once found in Mainland Asia, Europe, and Africa, but now restricted to a few islands in Malaysia, Indonesia, and the southern Philippines.

DIET CLASSIFICATION:
Carnivore

FOOD SOURCE:
Insects, frogs, lizards, small birds, bats, sometimes snakes

Tarsier tails are twice as long as they are! Good thing they can curl it up like this...

ANIMAL FACTS:

* The Tarsier is a tiny monkey who lives in the jungles of Southeast Asia. Their heads and bodies range from about four to six inches in length, which is about the size of a Chipmunk. The hind limbs are about twice this long, including the feet, and they also have a slender tail from about eight to ten inches long. Their fingers are <u>elongated</u>, with the third finger being about the same length as the upper arm. Most of the <u>digits</u> have nails, but the second and third toes of the hind feet have claws instead, which are used for grooming. Ouchy! I think that would hurt, don't you?

* They have very soft, velvety fur, which is generally brownish beige, or yellowish in color.

* Tarsiers tend to be extremely shy animals, and all Tarsier species are <u>nocturnal</u>, meaning that they are the most active at night.

WHAT MAKES THEM WEIRD & WACKY?

Tarsier monkeys are the only entirely <u>carnivorous</u> <u>primates</u> in the world. This means they don't eat any fruit or plants, only other creatures! They are primarily insect eaters and catch insects by jumping at them, often snatching their food out of mid-air with their sticky finger pads. They are also known to <u>prey</u> on birds, snakes, lizards, and bats.

They can turn their heads one hundred and eighty degrees in both directions, so they can see their <u>prey</u> without turning their bodies, kind of like a tiny owl...

They have large ears like a bat, and incredibly sensitive hearing, so they can hear their <u>prey</u> or <u>predators</u> coming. They have very long hind limbs, mostly because of the really long tarsal bones of the feet. In fact, that's where they get their name, the Tarsier Monkey.

This makes them uniquely suited for clinging to branches and leaping from that position, and enables them to jump more than forty times their own body length.
If we were able to do that, we would be able to jump the length of a football field, maybe almost two, which would make football A LOT more interesting, don't you think?

These monkeys are also different because they are much less <u>social</u> than most <u>primates</u>, preferring to live alone, or in small groups.

Tarsiers are best known for their unusually large eyes and actually have the BIGGEST eyes of any <u>mammal</u> on the planet, in relation to their body size. Each eyeball actually weighs more than the Tarsier's brain!

Does this mean that their brains are really, really small, or that their eyes are really, really big? I think it's probably both.

All the better to see you with, my dear....

WHY ARE THEY ENDANGERED?

Tarsiers are considered to be critically endangered, with possibly only a few hundred left. The biggest danger to them is loss of <u>habitat</u>, being hunted for food, and the exotic pet trade. I was thinking that I'd love to have a pet Tarsier until I found out that, unfortunately, Tarsiers do NOT do well in <u>captivity</u>, and many will actually commit suicide by bashing their heads against a wall until they die, sometimes within days of capture. That made me so sad!

FIELD ACTIVITY
Related to Tiny Monkeys Who Like to Eat Meat

Crickets are a favorite snack of Tarsier Monkeys. Did you know you can tell what the temperature is by a Cricket's chirp?

HERE'S HOW:

The male Cricket rubs his wings together to make the chirping sound. He does it to attract the ladies, or court a particular female. Sometimes, he does it as an aggressive act against other males, or to sound an alert when there's danger, like maybe when a Tarsier Monkey is around!

The frequency of chirping varies according to the temperature. To get the approximate temperature in degrees Fahrenheit, count the number of chirps in 15 seconds and then add 37. The number you get will be a rough estimate of the outside temperature.

Go out tonight and listen to a Cricket chirp. Do the math and then check a thermometer. Were you right? Or too high or too low? Practice makes perfect :)

Go have an
Noisy Night Adventure in YOUR neighborhood!

Come here, little buggy. I just want to talk to you!

Noooo. That wide-eyed, innocent look isn't fooling anybody...

Capybara

[kap-uh-bahr-uh]

BIGGEST. RAT. EVER.

A Capybara is out for a walk around the block. Nice neckerchief, dude.

Chillaxin' in the sun

Pig Prints

SCIENTIFIC NAME:
Hydrochoerus hydrochaeris

OTHER NAMES:
Meaning of name is "one who eats slender leaves" or "Grass Eater"

SPECIES CLASSIFICATION:
Mammal

IUCN STATUS:
LC – Least Concern

BIOME:
   Region: Central & Northern South America
   Habitat: Densely forested areas near water
   Range: About 50 acres for a group

DIET CLASSIFICATION:
Herbivore

FOOD SOURCE:
Grass and aquatic plants

Capy Families are happy families!

ANIMAL FACTS:

* The Capybara has a heavy, barrel-shaped body with reddish brown fur. It's about one and a half feet tall and about three to four feet in length.

* It has three large toes on its rear feet and four large toes on its front feet. And, even with those large-toed feet, it can run as fast as a horse!

* Big cats like Jaguars, Pumas, and Ocelots are the main predators of the Capybara, but also Eagles and Anacondas, too.

* No wonder it runs like a horse. So would I, wouldn't you?

* Capybaras live about eight to ten years, and have an average litter size of four babies.

WHAT MAKES THEM WEIRD & WACKY?

The Capybara's claim to fame is that it's the largest <u>rodent</u> in the world. It has been described as being "basically, a huge Guinea Pig." And, well...that's pretty much what it looks like.

BUT...unlike a Guinea Pig, it's also <u>semi-aquatic,</u> which means it's comfortable on land OR in the water.
It has webbed feet, and can keep most of its body <u>submerged</u>, like a Hippopotamus. It can squeeze its ears against its head to keep water out and can completely <u>submerge</u> itself for up to five minutes to hide from <u>predators,</u> which is a pretty cool trick.
But, can you imagine running as fast as a horse on webbed feet? Wow.

The Capybara's front teeth never stop growing. Like, ever. They have to wear them down by chomping on bark and wood, or they would trip over them eventually.

Some people keep them as pets, like the lady in the picture, even though they are wild animals.

And, here's a real Weird & Wacky thing:

MAMMAL OR FISH??

Apparently, people in Venezuela love eating Capybaras! They are considered to be such a delicacy, that they don't want to stop eating them during Lent, a Catholic religious season where you are not supposed to eat meat, unless it's a Fish. (Which is still meat, in my book, and my Goldfish, Einstein, agrees.) So, whoever was the Pope (the leader of the Catholic Religion) sometime in the 1500s, declared that the Capybara is a Fish, instead of a Mammal!
Um...no. If it gives birth to live offspring, is fur-bearing, and feeds its young with its own milk, IT IS A MAMMAL, Sir.
A MAMMAL, as plain as the stylin' hat on your head.

An Open Letter to the Pope:

Dear Pope,
Please don't change a Mammal into a Fish. Science doesn't work like that. Besides, isn't Lent about giving something up?
I respecfully suggest that people give up eating Capybaras.

Sincerely,
Cap Y. Bara

P.S. I really like your hat.

FIELD ACTIVITY
Related to a Hippo Pig who's a Social Butterfly

The super fun thing about Capybaras are that some species like to use them as chairs. Birds, monkeys, rabbits, turtles, even other Capybaras have been photographed lounging on top of them.

There's even a few websites and a Blog devoted to these pictures called, "Animals Sitting on Capybaras."

I'm not kidding. Apparently, Capybaras are so friendly and social, that not only do they get along great with humans, but all kinds of other species as well! We could certainly learn some lessons from the Capybara, couldn't we?

Below are some of the pictures I found. They're hysterical! I also made one of my own with my dog Jack. It's a fake. Jack has never met a Capybara. Can you draw an animal (or your brother, sister, Mom, Dad, teacher) sitting on a Capybara? You'll find a printable one at www. WeirdandWackyPlanet.com in the Downloads section.

Now, go out and have a
Party Animal Adventure in YOUR neighborhood!

This is a fake picture I made of Jack sitting on a Capybara. → She wishes it was real.

Mara

[mahr-uh]

THE KANGABIT OR THE RABBIROO?

This Mara is resting, because it needs to, after trying to be 3 or 4 different animals. I'm sure that's exhausting.

Stick your butt in the air like you don't care.

Hare Prints

SCIENTIFIC NAME:
Dolichotis patagonum

OTHER NAMES:
Patagonian Mara, Patagonian Cavy, Patagonian Hare or Dillaby.
Name means "Long Eared", but I wasn't that impressed by its ear length, really.

SPECIES CLASSIFICATION:
Mammal

IUCN STATUS:
NT – Near Threatened

BIOME:
Region: South American
Habitat: Coarse grassland, scrub desert, forests
Range: Argentina

DIET CLASSIFICATION:
Herbivore

FOOD SOURCE:
Grasses and other vegetation

"Are you my Mother??"

ANIMAL FACTS:

* Maras have stocky bodies with three sharp claws on their hind feet and four sharp claws on their front feet. They have brown fur on their heads and bodies with darker rumps and white bellies. Because their back legs are longer than their front legs, it looks like they walk around with their butts in the air all the time!

* They are about eighteen inches high and weigh around twenty-four pounds. That's bigger than your average Rabbit and more like the size of a Raccoon.

* They can run up to eighteen miles per hour, and their main predators are cats, foxes, and birds of prey.

* Maras live from seven to ten years and have one to three offspring per year.

WHAT MAKES THEM WEIRD & WACKY?

Maras are the fourth largest <u>rodent</u> in the world and, like the Capybara, are also close relatives of the Guinea Pig.

But, they have some weird, un-<u>rodent</u> like behaviors, like sunbathing, for instance. They like to lay around and take naps in the warm afternoon sun. I mean, who doesn't, right?

Maras can leap up to six feet, hop on their longer hind legs like a rabbit or kangaroo, bounce on all four legs, or gallop like a horse.

I'm not sure what other animal can do all of that!

They also mate for life, and rear their young in a communal <u>creche</u>, meaning that all the babies in the colony are located in one place and the adults take turns babysitting them.

Maras can be social with humans if raised that way from a young age, but they avoid people in the wild. They may even change from being day (<u>diurnal</u>) creatures to night (<u>nocturnal</u>) creatures, just to avoid social interaction with humans.

I know some people who are like this, too.

WHO ARE THE WORLD'S LARGEST RODENTS?

<u>Rodents</u> are <u>mammals</u> of the order Rodentia, and represent about 40% of all mammalian <u>species</u>. They are found on all continents, with the exception of Antarctica, and they live in a wide variety of <u>habitats</u>. They can be <u>arboreal</u>, <u>semi-aquatic</u> or <u>fossorial</u> in nature. They are characterized by a pair of constantly growing front teeth, both in the upper and lower jaws.
Some common household pets are <u>Rodents</u>, like Mice, Rats, Guinea Pigs, Hamsters, Chinchillas, Gerbils, and Rabbits.

The top 5 biggest Rodents in the world are as follows:
1. Capybara
2. Beaver
3. Cape Porcupine
4. Patagonian Mara
5. Bosavi Wolly Rat (He's as big as a cat)

FIELD ACTIVITY
Related to the Patagonian Guinea Rat

Maras are animals who exhibit what is called <u>Creche</u> Behavior. This means that they have a communal area where they keep all the babies, and the adults take turns babysitting them.

There are other animals who use this form of "it takes a village" child rearing, as well. Most of the species are birds, like Cormorants, Flamingos, Ducks, Ostriches, and Penguins.
But, there are fish who do it, like Catfish, and <u>mammals</u> who also do it, like Lions, Wild Dogs, and...Humans. Whaaaat??? Yes, Humans.
Have you ever attended daycare? Do you go to school? Have you ever had someone babysit you when your parents were away, either for the evening or longer? That means YOU have participated in <u>Creche</u> Behavior, too! The next time your Babysitter comes over, tell them they are in charge of the <u>Creche</u> (pronounced kresh) and see the look on their face, hahaha!

These aren't even my kids.

Mama!

Go have a
**Babysitting
Adventure**
in YOUR neighborhood!

Water Deer

BAMBI WITH FANGS

What a sweet little deer!
With full-on fangs.

Roe Deer
Prints

Pretty sure this one
is stuffed :(

32

SCIENTIFIC NAME:
Hydropotes inermis

OTHER NAMES:
Vampire Deer

SPECIES CLASSIFICATION:
Mammal

IUCN STATUS:
VU – Vulnerable

BIOME:
Region: Korea, China
Habitat: Tall reeds and grass areas
Range: Now also found in Britain, because of escapees and deliberate releases by man.

DIET CLASSIFICATION:
Herbivore

FOOD SOURCE:
Coarse grass

The female Water Deer has no fangs, but she is still sassy!

ANIMAL FACTS:

* Water Deer are small, Asian deer with yellowish-brown coats on their head and torso, and yellowish-white bellies. They have no rump patch or antlers, like most deer.

* They are about two to three feet long, and weight around twenty to thirty pounds. They look like they are about the size of an older fawn.

* Their main enemy is Man, through <u>poaching</u>, hunting, and <u>habitat</u> destruction.

* Water Deer live up to thirteen years and can have up to seven young at a time. They are the most <u>prolific</u> of all deer <u>species</u>, which means that they give birth to more babies at one time. Can you imagine seeing a Mother Deer with seven babies following behind her?!

WHAT MAKES THEM WEIRD & WACKY?

Ummm...they have FANGS!

Which is Weird and Wacky enough, all by itself, right?

But....those aren't actual fangs. They look like fangs, but are actually small tusks. They are the only species of deer where the males have no antlers. Instead, they have those long, curved, sharp tusks, which can exceed three inches in length.

They are also super good swimmers, which is why they're called Water Deer, and their hind legs are longer than their front legs, so they run in rabbit-like jumps.

Ok, back to the fangs.
They (the fangy-tusks) are movable in the sockets, and, by using facial muscles, can be moved out of the way to eat.

They can also be thrust out and prominently displayed for aggressive encounters with other males, and are only used for territorial fights, not for hunting.

Still, they are impressive looking. I wouldn't care to run into one in a dark forest, would you? I mean, whose idea was it to call them Water Deer? Shouldn't they be called Fang Faced Deer?

Are you Team Bambi or Team Deeracula?

HOW DID THEY GET TO GREAT BRITAIN?

The Chinese Water Deer were first brought to the London Zoo in 1873. Then, the Duke of Bedford, who was apparently a collector of deer, (odd hobby, right?) introduced them to his Woburn Estate in Bedfordshire. They first arrived in 1896, and he gave some to the nearby Whipsnade Park in 1929, now Whipsnade Zoo. Some escaped into the wild in 1945. No one is sure if they escaped from his estate or from Whipsnade Park, but, either way, they ran into the surrounding forest and began to have those "up to seven" offspring you read about earlier.
But here's the rub: no one is sure if this is a good thing or a bad thing. Usually, a species that is non-native to an area is considered an invasive species and does harm to the new ecosystem. This hasn't been the case so far. And, there is also this: the Chinese Water Deer are listed as Vulnerable on the IUCN list in their native China. About 10% of the population now resides in Great Britain, where they continue to thrive, while their numbers dwindle in China. So, no matter what, it looks like it was a good move for the Water Deer!

FIELD ACTIVITY

Related to Fang Faced Deer
(I changed their name.)

Even though Water Deer have obvious differences, they have a great deal in common with all species of Deer. Here are a few facts you may not have known :)

DEER FACTS TO STUN & AMAZE YOUR FAMILY & FRIENDS:

1. Most male Deer grow new antlers each year. (Water Deer do not.)

2. Animals such as Antelope resemble Deer in a number of ways, but have horns instead of antlers. The difference between them is that horns are not grown and replaced like antlers are.

3. During the mating season, male Deer will often use their antlers to fight for the attention of female Deer.

4. Most Deer are born with white spots to make them less visible to predators, but lose them within a year.

5. Deer can hear far better than humans. They can hear frequencies that humans can't. They can also turn their ears in any direction without turning their head.

6. Deer are excellent swimmers, even in deep water.

7. Deer also have extraordinary smelling ability. They can smell food from a large distance. They use this to communicate with each other, and also to detect the position of other groups of Deer.

8. Deer are more active in summer, and less active in winter. They also eat only one third of the food they usually eat, and stay in the woods to escape from the cold.

Go have a
Know-it-all Adventure
in YOUR neighborhood!

This is a real Chinese Water Deer skeleton from the Royal Veterinarian College in London.

And, you totally saw this part, right?

35

IN CONCLUSION

So there you have it. Eight of the Weirdest and Wackiest out there, in depth and up close and personal.

Are there more? Oh but, of course. I've only just begun. There are soooo many Weird and Wacky creatures out there, and more show up in my email every day.

Are they weirder than these? Most assuredly. The ocean has so many Weird and Wacky Creatures in it that I might have to split them into two, three, or maybe four books! Plus, wait till you see what the insect world has to offer. And, don't get me started on Camouflaged Creatures. They might be my favorites.....

If you'd like to vote on which book I'll write next, you can go to my website, www.WeirdandWackyPlanet.com and let me know which creatures you'd like to see in my next book.

Any ideas for Weird and Wacky creatures can be emailed to me from the contact form on the website. Some of my best ideas come from something a reader has suggested.

Don't forget to get your FREE downloads, because there are some surprises in there, and as always, remember that some of the best adventures are the ones you have in books. In fact, those are my very favorite kind!

Also, my dog, Jack says Hello.

Now, go have an adventure in YOUR neighborhood!

K.B. Carr, Adventuress
& Captain Jack, Sidekick

THANK YOU!

To thank you for reading this book, I have some free gifts for you!
To access your FREE Bonus Downloads for this book, go to
www.WeirdandWackyPlanet.com/wwcbonus92060.
I hope you enjoy them:)

ABOUT SCHOOL AUTHOR VISITS

Jack and I love to visit kids at their schools and talk about things like the animals in our books, how to write a book, or what kids can do to help the animals on our planet, especially the ones who are in trouble.

If you'd like us to visit YOUR school, just email me the name of your school, town and state, and I'll send an author visit packet to the appropriate person. And, who knows? Maybe someday, Jack and I will get to meet you in person!

ABOUT THE AUTHOR

K.B. CARR
   -Author and Accidental Adventuress

K.B. is an animal enthusiast, not an animal expert. They both start with the letter "e", but shouldn't be confused. One of them requires much larger student loans.

Her mother wanted to know why she asked so many questions all the time. "Curiosity killed the cat", her mother would say. "But, satisfaction brought her back", K.B. would reply.

She is the mother of two children, Ryan and Kelsey, and she tries really hard to answer all their questions if she can.

K.B. lives in West Michigan with her dog Jack.
Jack is a girl dog with a boy's name.

Human
Prints

K.B. says that Ryan, Kelsey, and Jack are -and always will be- her favorite Weird & Wacky Creatures.

ANIMAL INDEX

And, please don't forget to leave a review if you enjoyed it. I like to quote my favorite ones on book covers and social media. I might use yours! Plus, it helps me reach more readers who might enjoy this book, too.

GLOSSARY OF TERMS

Amphibian - any of a group of cold-blooded vertebrate animals (like frogs and toads) that have gills and live in water as larvae but breathe air as adults.

Aquatic - growing or living in or frequenting water.

Arboreal - living in or often found in trees.

Canines - a domestic dog or a related animal (like a wolf or fox) OR a pointed tooth next to the incisors.

Captivity - the state of being kept in a place (such as a prison or a cage) and not being able to leave or be free.

Carnivore/Carnivorous - an animal who eats the flesh of other animals.

Creche - a group of young animals (like penguins or bats) gathered in one place for care and protection, usually by one or more adults.

Crustacean - a type of animal (such as a crab or lobster) that has several pairs of legs and a body made up of sections that are covered in a hard outer shell.

Digits - a finger or toe.

Diurnal - active mainly during the day.

Domestic/Domesticated - to bring under the control of and make usable by humans. Cats and dogs are domesticated animals.

Elongate/Elongated - to make longer or to grow longer.

Extinct/Extinction - no longer existing.

Fossorial - an animal that is adapted to digging and life underground such as the Badger, the Naked Mole Rat, or the Star Nosed Mole.

Habitat - the environment an animal lives in, like deserts, marshes or forests.

Herbivore/Herbivorous - an animal that only eats plants.

Hybridization/Hybrid - to interbreed or combine species so as to produce a new species.

Invertebrates - lacking a spinal column.

Life span - the amount of time a person or animal actually lives.

Litter - the offspring at one birth.

Mammal - a type of animal that feeds milk to its young and that usually has hair or fur covering most of its skin, but not always, as in the case of marine mammals.

Nocturnal - active mostly at night.

Offspring - the child or young of a particular human, animal, or plant.

Omnivore - an animal that lives on a diet of both plant and animal food.

Poaching - hunting illegally and without permission.

Predator/Predators - an animal that hunts other animals for food.

Prehensile - adapted for seizing or grasping.

Prey - to hunt for animals that are food or referring to animals that are food.

Primate - any animal in the category of mammals that includes humans, monkeys, apes, and some smaller, simpler animals.

Prolific - producing young or new growth in abundance; fertile.

Range - the amount of land or territory that an animal is found in, like acres or countries.

Region - the area of the world an animal lives.

Rodent - type of gnawing, nibbling mammal, characterized by four continually growing front teeth.

Semi-aquatic - living near or spending time in water, such as otters.

Social - friendly; enjoying the company of others.

Solitary/Solitude - alone; without the company of others.

Species - a group of living things that are the same in many important ways. Members of a species can produce young together.

Submerge/Submerged - to be underneath water or beneath sand or such substance.

Tentacles - slender, flexible appendages used for touching or grabbing.

REFERENCES & PHOTO CREDITS

STAR NOSED MOLE:
PHOTOS: Dr. Ken Catania,gordonramsaysubmissions,Brandon Motz,Joanne Goldby, KB Carr
RESOURCES: http://en.wikipedia.org/wiki/Star-nosed_mole
http://www.biokids.umich.edu/critters/Condylura_cristata
http://www.naturalhistorymag.com/picks-from-the-past/201397/a-star-is-born

BABIRUSA:
PHOTOS: Eric Kilby,wolfsavard,Schristia,Masteraah,Didier Descouens,BioDiv Library
RESOURCES: http://en.wikipedia.org/wiki/Babirusa
http://www.arkive.org/sulawesi-babirusa/babyrousa-celebensis
http://www.wired.com/2014/05/the-creature-feature-10-fun-facts-about
-the-babirusa

OKAPI:
PHOTOS: Raul654,derekkeets,Kaelin,Irina Polikanova,Tambako the Jaguar
RESOURCES: http://a-z-animals.com/animals/okapi
http://en.wikipedia.org/wiki/Okapi
http://animals.sandiegozoo.org/animals/okapi

LIGER:
PHOTOS: aliwest44,Becker1999,Argusfoto,HKandy
RESOURCES: http://www.ligerfacts.org
http://a-z-animals.com/animals/liger
http://en.wikipedia.org/wiki/Liger

TARSIER MONKEY:
PHOTOS: Mendhak, lanz, Unsplash
RESOURCES: http://a-z-animals.com/animals/tarsier
http://en.wikipedia.org/wiki/tarsier
http://www.tarsierfoundation.org

CAPYBARA:
PHOTOS: Maortizjr,Tambako the Jaguar,lorentey,Me in Me,Whistling in the Dark,
mohit3474,Murray Foubister,ferjflores,annalu060
RESOURCES: hhttp://en.wikipedia.org/wiki/Capybara
http://animals.sandiegozoo.org/animals/capybara
http://animalssittingoncapybaras.tumblr.com

MARA:
PHOTOS: Snowman Radio,generalizing,wwarby,Marie Hale,
Public Domain Pictures,ctrialtdileep
RESOURCES: http://en.wikipedia.org/wiki/Patagonian_mara
http://www.arkive.org/patagonian-mara/dolichotis-patagonum
http://www.dudleyzoo.org.uk/our-animals/patagonian-mara

WATER DEER:
PHOTOS: Snowy Owls,Bruce Lee,Momotarou2012,Mr.John Cummings,
Nick Goodrum Photography
RESOURCES: http://en.wikipedia.org/wiki/Water_deer
http://www.arkive.org/chinese-water-deer/hydropotes-inermis
http://www.britannica.com/EBchecked/topic/112801/Chinese-water-deer

Made in the
USA
Middletown, DE